Tea with the Bennets
of Jane Austen's Pride and Prejudice

An Anthology of Recipes by
Margaret Vaughan

Printed in England

For my sisters
Jenny, Marian, Mary, Ann, Betty and Isobel

Contents

Introduction

This little book was written, in part, many years ago when I was first introduced to the Bennet family in Jane Austen's *Pride and Prejudice* by my English mistress. Being the youngest of seven girls I was, even then, drawn by the similarities between my own sisters and the Bennet girls. I well remember wondering if they, like us, had to do their share of the cooking ~ I obviously chose to ignore their mother's reply to Mr. Collins who, having praised the very fine dinner, begged to know to which daughter the excellence of its cookery was owing: *'But here he was set right by Mrs. Bennet, who assured him with some asperity that they were well able to keep a good cook, and that their daughters had nothing to do in the kitchen.'*

My interest was reawakened when part of the BBC's excellent 1995 adaptation of *Pride and Prejudice* was filmed in my home village of Lacock in Wiltshire (the little town of Meryton in the book). I decided to look out my original scribblings and add my latest ideas. As I have always been fascinated by the origins and development of indigenous recipes through the ages, I have so enjoyed letting my culinary imagination run riot from the Bennet's table to my own.

Throughout Jane Austen's novels the table was an important setting, the focus of much of the social life of the period. Guests were invited to dinner or supper, invitations accepted ~ important rituals which helped to reinforce a family's wealth and social standing and an intrinsic part of the plot.

Thankfully this custom remains today, although the cooking techniques may have changed. Unlike the Bennets, not many of us have our own cook and family members have to take their turn in the kitchen. We certainly did and at an early age learnt the rudiments and basic skills of cooking for a family (in my case nine of us).

King John's Hunting Lodge, Lacock

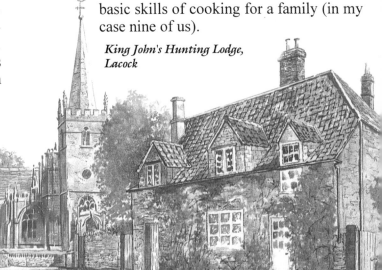

Tea with the Bennets

Not only am I one of seven girls but we are each named after one of my father's seven sisters, all of whom were good cooks. Indeed I still use many of their recipes in my tea-room, King John's Hunting Lodge.

I am just old enough (truly only just!) to remember cooking on an open fire at a very early age. My dear mother was very proud of her burnished black range and later her "modern" Triplex grate, and much, much later her Aga. I well remember the difficulty of getting the fire, and hence the oven, to the right heat and keeping the temperature constant for long enough to cook a meal. I must have enjoyed myself for I soon learnt not to be too timid a cook and to have fun.

Mrs. Bennet is proud that she keeps a *'very good table'* and uses her dinner parties to show off her daughters with all the social skills and foibles of the time. Teatime sometimes immediately followed on from dinner (now our lunchtime). Cook would produce all kinds of dishes for the side table as well as the main table using recipes handed down from family to family, cook to cook, even sister to sister.

Would Jane, Lizzy, Mary, Kitty or Lydia have had a recipe book ready for their cook? In our family, recipes were certainly shared and many have been handed down for at least three generations ~ some may even date back to the Bennet's own lifetime!

I am told I have a habit of describing people in culinary terms. I certainly find myself doing this with Mr. and Mrs. Bennet's family, friends and acquaintances. These are only my personal interpretations but you must surely agree that *Simpering Cake* could only be attributed to Mr. Collins, *Brittle Bites* to Lady Catherine de Bourgh and *Indelicate Pudding* to the impetuous, insensitive Lydia.

I have enjoyed my cookery journey with this delightful family. The comparisons between my own sisters and the Bennet girls have brought back happy memories of wonderful meals around our fine table prepared by one or other of us ~ a real time of sharing.

I hope you will enjoy trying some of these old and new recipes, even if you have no Mr. Collins to appreciate the *"Heavenly Pudding"* or *"Simpering Cake"*!

Daily Bread

This is definitely a loaf for the table at Pemberley. Bread was very much the staple food of the time, served at every meal of the day and "baking day" would have been a daily event in Darcy's time.

A High Class Loaf

(Makes 1 large or 3 small loaves)

25g/1oz. fresh yeast or 1¹/₂ tspn dried yeast
5mls/1 tspn sugar
1.4kg/3lbs. strong white flour or
675g/1¹/₂lbs. strong white flour and 675g/1¹/₂lbs. wholemeal flour
10mls/2 tspn vegetable oil
900ml/1¹/₂ pints warm water
10mls/2 tspn salt
egg for glazing
15g/¹/₂oz. poppy seeds

☙ Cream the fresh yeast with a little warm water and the sugar. Alternatively, sprinkle the dried yeast over half a pint of the warm water and leave to froth.
☙ Sift the flour into a large warm bowl and add the frothing yeast mixture.
☙ Add the oil to remaining warm water with the salt and mix into the flour with a wooden spoon.
☙ Turn out onto a floured board and knead for ten minutes, rolling the dough into an elastic, springy ball.
☙ Cover the dough in a bowl with a plastic sheet and towel and leave in a warm airing cupboard for up to 2 hours. Knead it again and shape it to fit the greased tin(s). Leave to rise again in a warm place for another hour.
☙ Egg wash the top and sprinkle with the poppy seeds. Make a shallow lengthways cut down the centre of the top and bake for 40 ~ 45 minutes in a pre-heated oven at 450ºF/230ºC/Gas Mark 8 (turn it down to a medium heat after 10 minutes). Remove from tins and allow to cool on a wire rack.

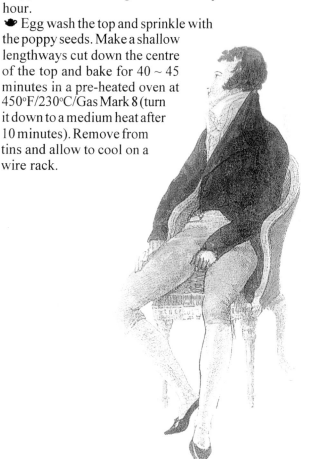

Wholemeal Bread

(A very significant loaf)
(Makes two 900g/2lb or four 450g/1lb loaves)

50g/2oz. fresh yeast or 3 level tspn dried yeast
15mls/1 level tblspn caster sugar
15-20mls/3-4 level tspn salt
1.4kg/3lbs. wholemeal flour
25g/1oz. lard
900ml/1¹/₂ pints warm water

 Blend the yeast into half a pint of the warm water in a small bowl. Alternatively, sprinkle the dried yeast over the warm water and set aside until frothy, then stir.

 Sift the flour, sugar and salt into a warm bowl. Cut up the lard and rub gently into the flour with your finger tips until it resembles fine breadcrumbs. Make a well in the centre and pour in yeast mixture. Add the remaining water.

 Using your hands work the mixture together thoroughly until it leaves the sides of the bowl clean.

 Turn out onto a floured board and knead for ten minutes, rolling the dough into an elastic, springy ball. Put in a warm place in a lightly oiled polythene bag until it doubles its size in about 2 hours.

 Turn the dough out onto a lightly floured surface and knead it again until firm. Divide it into two or four equal pieces and flatten each piece firmly with the knuckles to knock out any air bubbles. Stretch and roll each piece into an oblong the same length as the tin and then fold it into 3 along its width. Place into the greased tins and brush the tops with lightly salted water.

 Put each tin in a lightly oiled polythene bag. Tie the bags loosely and leave in a warm place for the dough to rise again until it fills the tins (about another hour). Remove the tins from the bags. Place them on a baking tray and bake for about 30 minutes (longer for the 2lb loaves) in a pre-heated oven at 450°F/230°C/Gas Mark 8, until the loaves shrink from the sides of the tins and are browned.

 Remove from tins and allow to cool on a wire rack. Test by tapping them ~ they should sound hollow.

Cheese Bread

25g/1oz. fresh yeast or 7.5mls/1$^1/_2$ tspn dried yeast
900g/2lbs. strong white flour
75g/3oz. finely grated cheese
15g/$^1/_2$oz. salt
15g/$^1/_2$oz fat
450ml/$^3/_4$ pint warm water

🍵 Pre-heat the oven to 425°F/220°C/Gas Mark 7.

🍵 Disperse the yeast in the warm water.

🍵 Sift the flour into a warm bowl and add the cheese and the salt.

🍵 Cut the fat into small pieces and rub into the flour with your finger tips. Stir in the water and yeast and mix to form a smooth dough.

🍵 Cover the bowl with a cloth and leave to prove for an hour at room temperature, then knead for a few minutes and leave to prove for a further half hour.

🍵 When proved, knead the dough into several balls. Put them into a greased bread tin and leave to prove for half an hour again.

🍵 Bake for 30 minutes. Remove from the tin and allow to cool on a wire rack.

Daily Bread

Soda Bread

150g/5oz. strong white flour
450g/1lb. wholemeal flour
50g/2oz. oatmeal
2.5mls/$\frac{1}{2}$ level tspn salt
5mls/1 tspn baking powder
600ml/1 pint sour milk

- Sieve all the dry ingredients together into a bowl.
- Make a well in the centre and stir in enough milk to make a fairly soft dough. Mix lightly and quickly with a wooden spoon.
- Turn onto a floured board and knead gently until smooth and free from cracks. Form into a round, place on a greased baking sheet and cut a large cross in the surface with a sharp knife.
- Bake in a pre-heated oven at 425°F/220°C/Gas Mark 7 for 30-45 minutes, until brown (Pierce the centre with a thin skewer to test for readiness: it should come out clean).
- Buttermilk or whey are equally good substitutes for the sour milk and would certainly have been much used in Mrs. Bennet's kitchen.

Crumpets

(Makes about 12)

300ml/10fl.oz. milk
50ml/2fl.oz. water
15mls/1 tblspn dried yeast
5mls/1 tspn caster sugar
225g/8oz. strong plain flour
5mls/1 tspn salt
butter for greasing

 Heat the milk and water together in a small saucepan until hand hot. Pour into a jug, stir in the sugar and dried yeast and leave in a warm place for 10-15 minutes.

Sift the flour and salt into a mixing bowl. Make a well in the centre and when the yeast mixture is frothy pour it in. Use a wooden spoon to gradually work in the flour and then beat well to make a smooth batter.

Cover the basin and leave in a warm place for 45 minutes. The batter will then be frothy.

Use a thick based frying pan or griddle and crumpet rings (usually about 10 cm. diam.) and grease the insides well. Place the pan over a medium heat for a few minutes, place 4-5 crumpet rings on and spoon some batter into each ring until it is 3-4 mm deep. Let them cook for 4-5 minutes. Holes will appear on the surface. Remove the rings, turn the crumpets over and cook the other side for 1 minute only. Transfer carefully to a wire rack to cool. Reheat the pan and repeat the cooking process for the remaining batter.

Toast the crumpets before serving and spread generously with butter.

Wednesday Scones

(Treacle Griddle Scones)

225g/8oz. plain flour
a pinch of salt
5mls/1 level tspn Cream of Tartar
5mls/1 level tspn baking powder
1.25mls/$\frac{1}{4}$ tspn cinnamon
15-20mls/1 large tblspn black treacle
150mls/$\frac{1}{4}$ pint milk (approx)

Sieve all the dry ingredients together into a bowl and make a well in the centre.

Slightly warm the treacle and put it in the well.

Pour the milk onto the treacle and gradually draw in the flour to make a fairly soft dough.

Turn onto a floured board and knead very slightly until smooth and free from cracks. Roll out into two rounds about half an inch thick and then divide each into four equal segments.

Place the segments on a hot, lightly greased griddle. When the underside has browned, turn over and continue cooking until cooked through (about 4 to 5 minutes). Allow to cool, wrapped in a cloth on a wire tray.

Daily Bread

Everyday Scones

50g/2oz. white flour
150g/6oz. wholemeal flour
2.5mls/$^1/_2$ level tspn salt
15mls/1 tblspn baking powder
50g/2oz. butter or margarine
150mls/$^1/_4$ pint milk (approx)

🍵 Sieve all the dry ingredients together into a bowl and then rub in the butter or margarine gently with your finger tips until the mixture resembles fine breadcrumbs.

🍵 Make a well in the centre and stir in enough milk to make a fairly soft dough.

🍵 Turn onto a floured board and knead very slightly until smooth and free from cracks. Cut into two and pat out with your hand to form two rounds about three quarters of an inch thick and then divide each into four equal segments.

🍵 Place the segments on a baking sheet and bake towards the top of a pre-heated oven at 450°F/230°C/ Gas Mark 8 for 8 - 10 minutes, until brown and well risen. Transfer to a wire rack to cool.

Sunday Scones

225g/8oz. white flour
2.5mls/$^1/_2$ level tspn salt
15mls/1 tblspn baking powder
50g/2oz. butter or margarine
25g/1oz. washed currants
150mls/$^1/_4$ pint milk (approx)

🍵 Sieve all the dry ingredients together into a bowl and then rub in the butter or margarine gently with your finger tips until the mixture resembles fine breadcrumbs. Stir in the currants.

🍵 Make a well in the centre and stir in enough milk to make a fairly soft dough.

🍵 Turn onto a floured board and knead very slightly until smooth and free from cracks. Cut into two and pat out with your hand to form two rounds about three quarters of an inch thick and then divide each into four equal segments.

🍵 Place the segments on a baking sheet and bake towards the top of a pre-heated oven at 450°F/230°C/ Gas Mark 8 for 8 - 10 minutes, until brown and well risen. Transfer to a wire rack to cool.

What a wonderful way to spend a cold afternoon ~ toasting cheese muffins for tea. Cook would have had a few hidden away for Mr. Bennet's solitary stints in the library, a useful (and comforting) means of escaping his wife's hysterical outbursts. I hope this is not necessarily the reason for their popularity in my Tea Rooms but they are certainly great tasty comforters.

Cheese Muffins

50g/2oz. lard
900g/2lbs. strong white flour
450g/1lb. grated cheese
pinch of salt
50g/2oz. fresh yeast or 3 level tspn dried yeast
600ml/1 pint warm water

🍴 Cut the lard into little pieces and place in a large bowl. Sieve in the flour, add grated cheese and salt and use your fingertips to mix the ingredients together.

🍴 Disperse the yeast in the warm water and add to the mixture to make a dough. Knead it and then let it rest for ten minutes.

🍴 Roll out the dough mixture on a lightly floured surface to half an inch thickness and cut into approximately 15 four-inch rounds.

🍴 Place on a lightly greased baking tray and bake in a pre-heated oven for 20 minutes at 400°F/200°C/Gas Mark 6. Allow to cool on a wire rack. To serve, cut in half horizontally and toast them on both sides. Spread liberally with butter or Gentlemen's Relish.

Side Table

Rather tedious and verbose, her head constantly in a book, Mary certainly needed a little spice and tartness in her life to sharpen her up. Between her pontifications I'm sure she would have enjoyed a spiced beef with pickled damsons, or perhaps a Surly Curd Tart might have suited her better. This is an old farming recipe.

Surly Curd Tart

1 pastry flan
1.1 litres/2 pints milk
5 mls/1 tsp. Epsom Salts
grated rind of one lemon
50g/2oz currants (optional)
25g/1oz butter
100g/4oz caster sugar
2 eggs, size 2
pinch of nutmeg

🍵 Have to hand an 8 inch uncooked pastry flan case.

🍵 Make 225g/8oz curd by heating, without allowing to boil, 2 pints of milk with 1 teaspoon of Epsom Salts. It will look slightly curdled. Strain through a fine sieve. The contents of the sieve will be the curd.

🍵 Mix the curd with the fruit and lemon rind.

🍵 Beat the butter and sugar together.
Beat the eggs separately and stir into the butter and sugar. Gently stir in the curd and then fill the pastry flan case with the mixture.

🍵 Bake in the oven at 350°F/180°C/Gas Mark 4 for about 20 minutes until set and slightly browned. Sprinkle with the nutmeg and serve.

Granny's Cheese Pudding

50g/2oz soft white breadcrumbs
1 good sized onion, finely chopped
2 tblspn chopped parsley or wild garlic (Jack by the hedge) or chives
salt and pepper to season
100g/4oz grated cheese
2 eggs
300ml/¹/₂ pint of milk
¹/₂ tspn dry mustard

🍵 Mix the breadcrumbs with the finely chopped onion and chopped herbs. Add 75g/3oz of the cheese. Put the mixture into a 1 pint greased dish or divide into four smaller ones.

🍵 Warm the milk slightly, beat the eggs and mustard into it with the seasoning and pour evenly over the breadcrumbs.

🍵 Sprinkle the remaining cheese on the top and leave to stand for 30 minutes.

🍵 Put hot water in a roasting tin until it is about one third full and then place the dish(es) into it. Bake in a pre-heated oven for 45-60 minutes at 400°F/200°C/Gas Mark 6.

Side Table

Lizzy could fill almost an entire cookery book but she does fall short on some of the niceties and sweetmeats. Not always correct in her assumptions she holds many surprises. A sharp apple and honey tart lined with (surprise, surprise) cheese pastry, that's Lizzy - savoury and sweet in one. My eldest sister was just like that. She was also a great cook, brooked no nonsense, was witty, made many instant and sometimes quite erroneous judgements but was quick to apologise when proved wrong. She was very beautiful with a strong personality, just like Lizzy.

Sharp Apple & Honey Tart

225g/8oz plain flour
75g/3oz margarine
2.5ml/$\frac{1}{2}$ tspn salt
100g/4oz strong cheese
water to mix
450g/1lb tart cooking apples
15ml/1 good tblspn honey
milk to glaze pastry

🍵 Make the pastry in the usual way by sifting the flour into a bowl with the salt and gently rubbing in the margarine until the mixture resembles fine breadcrumbs.

🍵 Finely grate the cheese and stir it into the flour. Add sufficient water to make a good pastry.

🍵 Peel, core and slice the apples for the filling.

🍵 Use half the pastry, rolled out, to line a greased 9 inch plate. Add the apples and the honey and cover with the other half of the pastry, joining the edges in the usual way, using any spare pieces to decorate the top with the shapes of leaves.

🍵 Brush with milk and bake at 375°F/190°C/ Gas Mark 5 for 20-30 minutes.

Potato Scones

225g/8oz cold cooked potatoes
15g/$\frac{1}{2}$oz melted butter
good pinch of salt
50g/2oz plain flour
lard to grease the griddle

🍵 Mash the potatoes thoroughly then mix in the salt and melted butter.
🍵 Gradually beat in the flour to form a soft dough.
🍵 Divide the dough into two. On a lightly floured surface, roll out each one into a round 3-4mm thick. Cut each round into four equal quarters.
🍵 Lightly grease a hot griddle and cook the scones on each side until golden brown. Wrap in a cloth to cool.

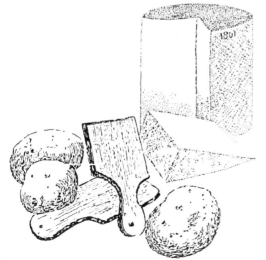

Cheese & Parsley Custard Pudding

2 eggs
300 ml/$\frac{1}{2}$ pint of milk, luke warm
75g/3oz grated cheese
50g/2oz soft white breadcrumbs
$\frac{1}{2}$ tspn dry mustard
$\frac{1}{2}$ tspn salt
2 tblspn chopped parsley or Wild Garlic

🍵 Separate the eggs. Beat the yolks in the luke warm milk with the cheese.
🍵 Mix the crumbs with the mustard, salt and parsley. Gradually stir into the milk and leave to stand for 30 minutes.
🍵 Beat the egg whites until stiff and them fold them into the mixture.
🍵 Put in a greased 1 pint ovenware dish and bake for 30 minutes at 400°F/200°C/Gas Mark 6.
🍵 Alternatively, you could try this recipe using 50g/2oz finely chopped ham instead of the parsley.

Side Table

Cheese Straws

50g/2oz breadcrumbs
50g/2oz plain flour
50g/2oz grated cheese
50g/2oz butter
a little cayenne pepper and salt to season

☙ Mix all the ingredients well together and then roll out fairly thickly on a floured surface. Cut into thin strips about $1\frac{1}{2}$ cms by 12 to 15cms.

☙ Place on a greased baking sheet and bake in the middle of a hot oven at 400°F/200°C/ Gas Mark 6 for about 15 minutes. The straws should be crisp and pale golden brown like shortbread.

Celery & Cheese Savouries

25g/1oz butter
15g/$\frac{1}{2}$ oz flour
300ml/$\frac{1}{2}$ pint of milk
cayenne pepper, salt and nutmeg to season
$\frac{1}{2}$ breakfast cup of chopped, cooked celery
75g/3oz grated cheese
few thin slices wholemeal bread

☙ Melt the butter in a pan and stir in the flour. Gradually pour in the milk and add the seasoning.

☙ Stir in the celery and then add 50g/2oz of the cheese.

☙ Roll out thinly some slices of wholemeal bread and use them to line 12 small paté tins.

☙ Fill the lined tins two thirds full with the celery mixture and sprinkle with the remaining cheese.

☙ Bake for 15-20 minutes at 400°F/200°C/ Gas mark 6. Turn out the savouries and serve hot or cold.

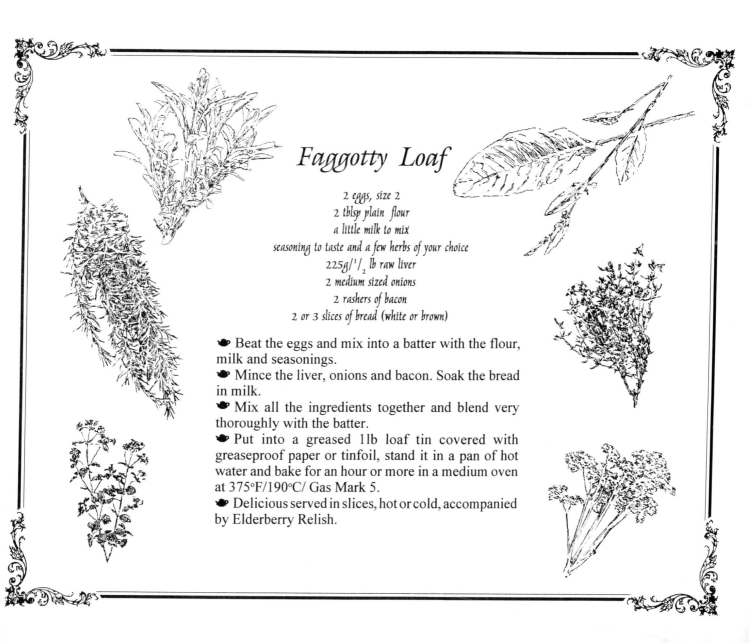

Faggotty Loaf

2 eggs, size 2
2 tblsp plain flour
a little milk to mix
seasoning to taste and a few herbs of your choice
225g/$\frac{1}{2}$ lb raw liver
2 medium sized onions
2 rashers of bacon
2 or 3 slices of bread (white or brown)

🍃 Beat the eggs and mix into a batter with the flour, milk and seasonings.

🍃 Mince the liver, onions and bacon. Soak the bread in milk.

🍃 Mix all the ingredients together and blend very thoroughly with the batter.

🍃 Put into a greased 1lb loaf tin covered with greaseproof paper or tinfoil, stand it in a pan of hot water and bake for an hour or more in a medium oven at 375°F/190°C/ Gas Mark 5.

🍃 Delicious served in slices, hot or cold, accompanied by Elderberry Relish.

Tea Table

Mrs Bennet found Kitty's persistent coughing most aggravating and constantly demanded her daughter to stop immediately! She would have been much wiser to administer blackcurrant tea or cordial. Herb teas were less expensive than Indian and, together with cordials, were much used for medicinal purposes. My own children loved blackcurrant cordial and my mother used lots of old remedies such as strap molasses to keep the winter chills at bay.

I still make Shepherd's Purse from an old farming family recipe. This rich treacle and chocolate concoction was made originally to keep the cold out on bleak lambing nights and today it's still a great winter treat. A slice or two would have done Kitty (and therefore her mother's nerves!) a power of good. I used to use strap molasses but have refined the recipe a little now I am no longer shepherding.

Shepherd's Purse

The Sponge

50g/2oz butter
45 mls/3 tblspn black treacle
2 eggs, size 2
100g/4oz self-raising flour
50g/2oz chopped walnuts
100g/4oz chocolate chips (or broken cooking chocolate)

🍃 Melt the butter with the treacle and allow to cool.
🍃 Add the eggs and whisk into the treacle mixture.
🍃 Gently fold in the flour, walnuts and chocolate chips.
🍃 Pour into a swiss roll tin lined with greaseproof paper and bake for 20-25 minutes at 375°F/190°C/Gas Mark 5. Allow to cool slightly and turn out onto a wirre cooling rack.

The Topping

100g/4oz butter
175g/6oz icing sugar
15 mls/1 tblespn black treacle

🍃 Sieve the icing sugar into a bowl. Add the softened butter and cream together with a wooden spoon until smooth. Add the treacle and mix thoroughly (add more treacle according to taste!)

🍃 Cover the cool sponge mixture with the topping and cut into 12 to 16 pieces.

Rich Chocolate Cake

The Cake

100g/4oz plain flour
25g/1oz cocoa
2.5mls/¹/₂ level tspn bicarbonate of soda
2.5mls/¹/₂ level tspn salt
150g/5oz caster sugar
50g/2oz quick creaming margarine
¹/₂ teacup of milk
1 egg/size 2

☙ Sift the flour, salt, bicarbonate and cocoa into a basin. Add the margarine in slices, the sugar, egg and milk.
☙ Blend them all together with a wooden spoon and then whisk until the mixture is smooth and light.
☙ Divide into 2 greased and lined 20cm/8 inch sandwich tins and spread level. Bake for 25 minutes at 375°F/190°C/Gas Mark 5. Cool before turning out.

The Icing

75g/3oz icing sugar
25g/1oz cocoa
40g/1¹/₂ oz butter
30 mls/2 tblspns water
50g/2oz caster sugar
¹/₂ tspn vanilla essence
lemon marmalade or apple jelly

☙ Sift the icing sugar and cocoa into a basin.
☙ Put the butter, water, caster sugar and vanilla essence into a saucepan and stir over a low heat. Just bring to the boil and remove from the heat at once. Pour into the centre of the dry ingredients and beat with a wooden spoon until the mixture is smooth. Leave to cool, stirring occasionally, until the mixture is fairly thick.
☙ Upturn one of the cakes and spread a little icing over the bottom. Spread the bottom of the other one with the lemon marmalade or apple jelly and sandwich the two together.
☙ Spread the remainder of the icing all over the cake (including the sides) and allow to set.

Shearing Cake

The Cake

225g/8oz plain flour
100g/4oz butter
175g/6oz soft brown sugar
$^1/_2$ lemon
5 mls/1tspn baking powder
10 mls/2tspn caraway seeds
ground nutmeg
150 mls / $^1/_4$ pint milk
1 egg

🍵 Rub the butter into the flour until the mixture resembles fine breadcrumbs and then stir in the brown sugar.

🍵 Grate the rind of half a lemon. Add it to the mixture with the baking powder, caraway seeds and a good pinch of ground nutmeg.

🍵 Lightly beat the egg into the milk and stir this into the dry mixture.

🍵 Line a 20cm/8 inch round cake tin with buttered paper and put the mixture in it. Bake for 1 hour at 350°F/180°C/Gas Mark 4.

🍵 Remove from the oven and turn out onto a wire rack to cool.

The Icing

100g/4oz icing sugar
approx. 1 lemon

🍵 Meanwhile make the icing. Mix the icing sugar with sufficient lemon juice to make a running consistency and ice the top of the cake when cold. Sprinkle with rosemary sugar.

Rosemary Sugar

🍵 Clean and dry some sprigs of Rosemary. Place in a screw-topped jar and fill with caster sugar. Seal and shake well. Leave for 24 hours and shake well again. Leave for a week before using.

Tea Table

Cherry Cake

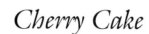

100g/4oz butter or margarine
100g/4oz caster sugar
2 eggs, size 2
few drops vanilla essence
175g/6oz flour
5 mls/1 level tspn baking powder
about 175g/6oz glace cherries

🍵 Cream the butter and sugar together until light and fluffy.

🍵 Whisk the eggs and add slowly to the butter mixture. If it shows signs of curdling add a little sifted flour. Add the vanilla essence.

🍵 Sieve the flour and baking powder and fold into the mixture gently with a metal spoon. Chop up the cherries and roll in flour. Add the cherries and milk to the mixture.

🍵 Pour into a greased and floured or lined 18-20 cm/ 7-8 inch round cake tin, level out the top and bake for about $1\frac{1}{4}$ hours at 325-350°F/160-180°C/ Gas Mark 3-4.

🍵 Test the cake before removing from the tin: ensure that it has shrunk away from the sides of the tin and is firm to the touch. Turn out onto a wire rack to cool.

Lydia's Ginger Curls

200g/7oz butter
225g/8oz demerara sugar
225g/8oz plain flour
5 ml/1 tsp ground ginger
$\frac{1}{4}$ nutmeg grated
250g/9oz golden syrup

🍵 Beat the butter to a cream with a whisk.
🍵 Fold in the sugar, flour, ginger and grated nutmeg.
🍵 Mix in the golden syrup to form a soft dough.
🍵 On a well floured board, roll the dough out thinly (about 3mm) and cut into strips about 2cms wide and 12 cms long. Place on a buttered and floured baking tray and bake in the oven at 350°F/180°C/Gas Mark 4 for 5-6 minutes. Remove from the oven and, before they get cold, curl each strip diagonally round the handle of a wooden spoon to produce a 'kiss curl' effect.

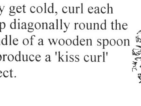

We have all met the likes of Mr Collins - gushing and pretentious without reason. This recipe for a tasty, everyday fruit cake aspires to a grandeur it doesn't quite attain!-

Simpering Cake

100g/4oz butter or margarine
100g/4oz caster sugar
2 eggs, size 2
225g/8oz self-raising flour or
225g/8oz plain flour with 2 level tspns baking powder
225g/8oz dried fruit
25-50g/1-2oz candied peel
90 mls/6 tblspn milk approx.
25-50g/1-2oz blanched almonds to decorate

🍵 Cream the butter and sugar together until light and fluffy.

🍵 Whisk in the eggs a little at a time. If the mixture shows signs of curdling, add a little sifted flour.

🍵 Sieve the remaining flour (and baking powder) and fold into the mixture gently with a metal spoon. Add the fruit and peel and enough milk to make a slow dropping consistency.

🍵 Pour into a greased and floured or lined 900g/2lb loaf tin and decorate the top with almonds. Bake for 1 to $1\frac{1}{4}$ hours at 350-375°F/180-190°C/ Gas Mark 4. Test before removing from the oven. The cake should have shrunk away from the sides of the tin and be firm to touch. A skewer inserted should come away clean.

Boiled Fruit Cake

450g/1lb mixed fruit
200g/7oz demerara sugar
240mls/8fl.oz water
100g/4oz margarine
10 mls/2 tspn mixed spice
2 eggs, size 2
125g/5oz self-raising flour
2.5 mls/$\frac{1}{2}$ tspn bicarbonate of soda

🍵 Place the fruit, sugar, water, margarine and spice into a saucepan, bring to the boil and simmer for 15-20 minutes. Pour into a mixing bowl and leave to cool.

🍵 Whisk the eggs, sift the flour and bicarbonate of soda and whisk together with the eggs.

🍵 Add to the fruit mixture and then pour into a greased and floured or lined cake tin and bake on the middle shelf for about $1\frac{3}{4}$ hours at 325°F/160°C/Gas Mark 3.

Cider Loaf Cake

350g/12oz mixed dried fruits
300 mls/¹/₂ pint of sweet cider
2 large eggs
275g/10oz self-raising flour
75g/3oz chopped cob nuts
175g/6oz brown sugar
grated rind of one orange

Lemon Cake
(or Orange or Lime)

2 lemons
2 eggs, size 2
100g/4oz butter
175g/6oz caster sugar
175g/6oz self-raising flour
approx. 60 mls/4 tblspns milk

❧ Place the fruit and cider in a bowl and leave to marinate overnight.

❧ When well soaked bring the cider and the fruit to the boil and then let it cool.

❧ Whisk the eggs briefly and then add them and all the other ingredients to the cider and fruit. Mix together and stir well.

❧ Turn into greased and floured tins (this quantity will make two 450g/1lb cakes). Bake for 1¹/₂ hours at 325°F/160°C/Gas Mark 3.

❧ Remove from the oven and turn out onto a wire rack to cool.

❧ Grate the rind of, and extract the juice from, the lemons. Beat the eggs.

❧ Whisk the butter, caster sugar and lemon rind together until fluffy then gradually beat in the eggs.

❧ Mix in the flour with a wooden spoon and add the milk a little at a time until the mixture is soft enough to drop off the end of the spoon when shaken gently.

❧ Grease a 900g/2lb loaf tin and turn the mixture into it.

❧ Bake in a moderate oven (350°F/180°C/Gas Mark 4) for 45-50 minutes until well risen and golden, firm on top and shrinking from the sides of the tin.

❧ Remove from the oven and whilst the cake is still warm, pierce the top all over with a skewer and pour on the lemon juice. Leave the cake in the tin until cold, so that all the juice is absorbed by the sponge.

❧ Turn out and wrap the cake in foil to keep it moist and fresh until needed.

Honey Buns

The Buns

100g/4oz caster sugar
100g/4oz butter
2 eggs, size 2
175g/6oz self-raising flour
5 mls/1 tspn clear honey
15 mls/1tblspn milk

🐝 Cream the butter and sugar together until light in colour.

🐝 Whisk the eggs and then add them to the butter and sugar, adding a little flour if the mixture shows signs of curdling.

🐝 Stir in the flour and then add the honey and milk gradually until the consistency of the mixture will just drop off the spoon.

🐝 This will fill about 20 bun tins or cases. Bake for 15 minutes at 375°F/190°C/Gas Mark 5. Allow to cool.

The Icing

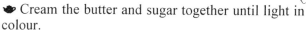

225g/8oz icing sugar
3 dessertspn clear honey
1 dessertspn mead or water

🐝 Beat all the ingredients together and then run the icing onto the buns.

🐝 These look particularly pretty decorated with crystalised violets or primroses.

Cornish Fairings

100g/4oz plain flour
pinch of salt
1.25mls/$\frac{1}{4}$ tspn ground ginger
1.25mls/$\frac{1}{4}$ tspn cinnamon
1.25mls/$\frac{1}{4}$ tspn mixed spice
7.5 mls/$1\frac{1}{2}$ tspn bicarbonate of soda
50g/2oz butter
50g/2oz caster sugar
7.5 mls/$1\frac{1}{2}$ level tspn golden syrup

🐝 Sift the flour, salt, ginger, cinnamon, spice and bicarbonate into a basin.

🐝 Rub the butter into the dry ingredients until the mixture resembles fine breadcrumbs. Mix in the sugar.

🐝 Melt the syrup and stir it into the mixture to make a soft dough.

🐝 Roll the mixture between the hands to make small balls about the size of marbles and place them on greased baking trays with a space between them to allow for spreading. Bake in the oven for 10 minutes at 350°F/180°C/Gas Mark 4.

🐝 Take the tray out of the oven and tap it on a solid surface in order to make the fairings crack and spread.

🐝 Put them back in the oven for a further 5 minutes to finish cooking.

"King John's" Hunter's Nuts

225g/8oz plain flour
5 mls/1 level tspn ground ginger
75g/3oz butter
175g/6oz sugar
50g/2oz finely chopped hazel nuts
1 small egg
75g/3oz black treacle

🍵 Sift the flour and the ginger into a bowl and then rub in the butter until the mixture resembles fine breadcrumbs.

🍵 Add the sugar and hazel nuts.

🍵 Beat the egg. Stir it into the mixture with the treacle.

🍵 Form into small balls about the size of marbles and place on a greased baking tray.

🍵 Bake for 30 minutes in a slow oven (325°F/160°C/ Gas Mark 3).

🍵 Leave to cool on the tray for 2-3 minutes before transferring carefully to a wire rack to cool.

Meryton Market Squares

The Biscuits

450g/1lb butter or margarine
225g/8oz caster sugar
2.5mls/$^1/_2$ tspn vanilla essence
450g/1lb self raising flour

🍵 Cream the butter and sugar together until light and fluffy.

🍵 Add the vanilla essence. Sieve the flour and fold into the mixture.

🍵 Put the mixture in a piping bag with a large star nozzle and pipe 2 inch squares by making three touching 2 inch lines side by side on a greased baking tray. Leave space between the squares and bake for 10-15 minutes at 325°F/160°C/ Gas Mark 3. Allow to cool slightly and transfer to a wire cooling rack.

The Filling

100g/4oz butter
450g/1lb icing sugar
few drops vanilla essence
water to soften

🍵 Cream all the ingredients thoroughly together.

🍵 When the biscuits are cold, sandwich them together in pairs with a little of the cream filling and dust with icing sugar.

"Lady Catherine de Bourgh's" Brittle Bites or Snaps

225g/ ¹/₂ lb butter
350g/ ³/₄ lb black treacle
100g/¹/₄ lb brown sugar
350g/³/₄ lb plain flour
2.5 mls/¹/₂ tspn bicarbonate of soda
15 mls/1 tbsp water

🍂 Place the butter and treacle in a saucepan and dissolve over a gentle heat. Allow to cool a little.

🍂 Mix the sugar and flour together in a basin, pour in the melted butter and treacle and mix well. Dissolve the bicarbonate of soda in a tablespoon of tepid water and add it to the mixture.

🍂 Well grease a baking tray and drop the mixture onto it a teaspoonful at a time, leaving room between each one for the biscuits to spread. Bake in a moderate oven (375°F/190°C/ Gas Mark 5) for about 10-15 minutes until nicely browned.

🍂 Leave for a few minutes then transfer to a wire rack to cool and crisp up. Store in an airtight tin.

Haw Jelly

haws
300mls/¹/₂ pint water and 1 lemon per pound of fruit
450g/1lb sugar per 600 mls/pint of strained juice

❧ Put the haws in a preserving pan with the water and add the juice, pips and rind of the lemon.

❧ Simmer until the haws are tender, stirring occasionally with a wooden spoon to break them up somewhat then strain through a jelly bag for several hours.

❧ Measure the juice and return to the pan with 450g/1lb of sugar per pint of juice. Dissolve the sugar and boil until setting point is reached. To test for this, drop a small spoonful of jelly onto a cold plate and allow to cool. The jelly is ready if a skin forms and wrinkles when a spoon is drawn across it.

❧ When ready, pour the jelly into clean, dry, hot jars. Place wax discs on top of each jar, cover and seal.

Rose-Geranium Jelly

1.15 kg/2¹/₂ lb crab apples or other hard cooking apples
1.1 litres/2 pints water
450g/1lb sugar for each pint of apple juice
a sprig of rose-geranium

❧ Chop up the apples coarsely including the cores and skins. Simmer in the water in a preserving pan, stirring occasionally, until the apples are completely softened. Strain through a jelly-bag (this may take several hours).

❧ Measure the juice and return to the pan with 450g/1lb of sugar per pint of juice. Dissolve the sugar and bring to the boil.

❧ Tie the rose-geranium in a small piece of cloth and suspend it in the boiling juice for two or three minutes. Continue boiling until setting point is reached. To test for this, drop a small spoonful onto a cold plate. When cool, draw a spoon across it - if set it should wrinkle.

❧ When ready, pour the jelly into clean, hot jars. Place wax discs on top of each jar then cover, seal and label.

❧ Growing rose-geraniums in the kitchen creates a wonderful scent. This jelly is delicious on fresh bread, scones and toast at tea-time.

Pear and Ginger Jam

1.6 kg/3$\frac{1}{2}$ lb pears
600 mls/1 pint water
1 large lemon or 2 small ones
$\frac{3}{4}$ inch fresh root ginger
1.15 kg/2$\frac{1}{2}$ lb sugar

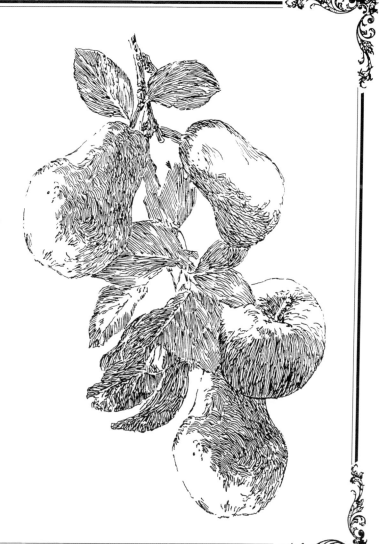

🍵 Peel and core the pears and chop them up (keep the peel and cores). Put the pears in a preserving pan or large saucepan with the water.

🍵 Grate the rind of the lemon and squeeze the juice. Crush the peeled root ginger with a rolling pin and then tie it in a piece of cloth or muslin with the lemon rind, pear peelings and cores. Suspend the bag in the pears and allow to simmer for about half an hour or so until the pears are well cooked and mushy.

🍵 Remove the pear peelings etc. Stir in the lemon juice and sugar until it has dissolved and then boil again for 15-20 minutes, stirring occasionally, until setting point is reached. To test for this, drop a small spoonful onto a cold plate. When cool, draw a spoon across it - if set it should wrinkle.

🍵 Skim the top of the mixture and then pour into hot jars. Place wax discs on top of each jar then cover, seal and label.

Quite honestly, in spite of her acknowledged beauty, Jane is a little too sweet for me at times. Saints are altogether too difficult to live with! She reminds me of all those light moulds and sweet delights that my children loved.

Elderflower, Lime or Lemon Posset

600 mls/1 pint of thick cream
150 mls/5 fl oz dry white wine
150 mls/5 fl oz elderflower cordial or
finely grated zest and juice of 2 limes or 2 lemons
30–45 mls/2-3 tblsp sugar
whites of 3 large eggs
fresh fruit to garnish

🍵 Whisk the cream in a large bowl until stiff. Stir in the dry white wine then whisk in the elderflower cordial or lemon or lime zest and juice.
🍵 Stir in the sugar to taste.
🍵 Whisk the egg whites until they form peaks and then fold gently into the cream mixture. Chill in the refrigerator.
🍵 Whisk the mixture again before serving in a dish or individual glasses. Garnish with elderflowers and/or lemon or lime slices.

Lydia, the youngest of the daughters, was a flibberti-gibbet of a girl with her head full of nonsense. Her elopement was a great calamity for the Bennet family. My recipe for "Indelicate Pudding" seems such an apt dish for Lydia and the rascally Mr Whickham. Their elopement was yet another like comparison with my sisters, one of whom eloped in what I considered at the time a truly romantic fashion. My father did not approve of the match, though for the life of me I cannot remember why, and he was to be proved very wrong.

My sister is a wonderful, all-round cook with the lightest of touches imaginable for pastries and sponges. I am of the opinion that happy and contented cooks have that rare, light touch. Eloping was to be my sister's path to happiness but I doubt if Lydia was quite so fortunate!

"Mr Whickham's" Indelicate Pudding

two 8-inch Vienna rolls
50g/2oz butter
100g/4oz caster sugar
3 satsumas
4 eggs, size 2
1.1 litres/2 pints milk
60 mls/2fl oz Grand Marnier
1 small orange
25g/1oz orange marmalade

🍵 Slice the Vienna rolls into half inch slices and butter them. Layer the bottom of a 1.1 litre/2 pint pie dish with half the bread and sprinkle with one third of the sugar.

🍵 Peel the satsumas and carefully remove the pith. Separate into segments and put one on each roundel of bread. Cover with a second layer of bread and sprinkle with sugar and a second layer of satsuma segments.

🍵 Whisk the eggs, add the milk and Grand Marnier and pour the mixture over the bread and satsumas. Place the dish in a bain-marie and bake in the oven at 325°F/160°C/Gas Mark 3 for 1 hour until set and golden brown.

🍵 Decorate the top with slices of the peeled orange and glaze the whole top with the warmed marmalade. Place under a hot grill for a few minutes to caramelize.

Baked Figs

A wonderfully quick and delicious dessert.
Allow 2 figs per person.

🍵 Core some apples - I try to use Coxes but any good, crisp eating apples will do. Leave the skins on and cut into 4mm slices so that there is a slice for each fig. Place the slices in an ovenproof or microwaveproof dish.

🍵 Cut a cross in the top of each fig and place one on each apple slice.

🍵 Pour into each fig half a teaspoonful of clear honey.

🍵 Bake in a fairly hot oven (375°F/190°C/Gas Mark 5) for 15-20 minutes or in the microwave on full power for about 3 minutes until just softened but still whole.

🍵 Serve with creme fraiche, whipped double cream or ice cream. Scrumptious!!

Snow Flip

1 teacup whole rice
150 mls/5fl oz whipping cream
15 mls/1tblspn caster sugar
vanilla essence

🍵 Boil the rice in water until soft. Drain and allow to cool.

🍵 Add the sugar and a few drops of vanilla essence to the cream and them whisk until stiff.

🍵 Fold the cream into the rice and whip together.

🍵 Pile the flip onto a dish and serve either on its own or with stewed fruit.

Almond and Raisin Pudding

75g/3oz suet

$^1/_2$ ground nutmeg

100g/4oz granulated sugar

175g/6oz breadcrumbs

2 eggs, size 2

150 mls/$^1/_4$ pint milk

almond flavouring

50g/2oz blanched almonds

175g/6oz stoned raisins

❧ Chop the suet and mix well with the nutmeg, sugar and breadcrumbs.

❧ Whisk the eggs with the milk and a few drops of flavouring. Mix into the dry ingredients.

❧ Well butter a 2 pint pudding basin and line the bottom and sides with the almonds and raisins. If there are any over, chop them up and add them to the mixture.

❧ Pour the mixture into the pudding basin, seal the top with greaseproof paper and tinfoil tied round with string and steam for 3$^1/_4$ hours. Turn out onto a serving plate and serve with a sweet sauce.

Apricot Cream

900 mls/1$^1/_2$ pints milk

1 small vanilla pod or a little vanilla essence

50g/2oz ground rice

50g/2oz apricot jam

15 mls/1 tablespoon hot water

25g/1oz caster sugar

❧ Bring the milk to the boil and add the vanilla pod or a little essence just before it reaches boiling point.

❧ Mix the ground rice to a smooth paste with a little water. Pour the milk over the paste, stir well and then slowly boil for a few minutes.

❧ Mix the jam with the hot water and pass through a fine sieve. Add to the rice and milk and stir in the sugar.

❧ Pour into a wetted mould and leave to cool and set. When quite cold, turn out onto a serving plate and serve with cream or custard.

Green Apple Fool

900g/2lb cooking apples
100-175g/4-6oz caster sugar
juice of 1 orange
300 mls/$\frac{1}{2}$ pint whipping cream
green colouring
4 savoy finger biscuits

🍵 Peel, core and slice the apples and cook in a double saucepan with the sugar and orange juice for approximately 20 minutes, stirring constantly. Allow to cool and then whisk for a minute or two.
🍵 Whisk the cream until just stiff. Fold into the cool apple purée and divide the mixture in half. Add a few drops of colouring to one half to make it a pale green.
🍵 Fill glasses with alternate layers of the plain and green purée. Serve topped with halved savoy finger biscuits.
Serves 4-6 people.

Lemon Dainty

2 eggs, size 2
15g/$\frac{1}{2}$oz butter
grated rind and juice of 1 lemon
60 mls/4 level tbspn granulated sugar
15 mls/1 level tbspn plain flour
320 mls/good $\frac{1}{2}$ pint milk

🍵 Separate the eggs and mix the yolks with the sugar, butter, flour, lemon rind and juice. Stir in the milk.
🍵 Whisk the egg whites until they just hold peaks and then fold into the mixture.
🍵 Pour into a buttered 1 pint dish and stand in a tin of hot water.
🍵 Bake in the oven at 375°F/190°C/Gas Mark 5 for about 20 minutes until the top is a delicate brown and just set.
🍵 This pudding is equally good cold and should have a spongy top with a sauce at the bottom.

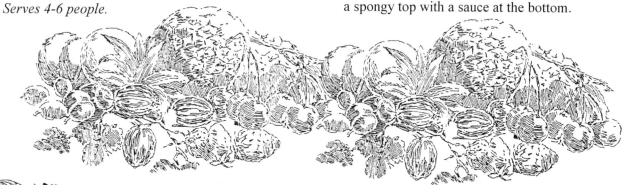

Orange Shape

3 oranges
100g/4oz caster sugar
$^1/_2$ small cup of water
50g/2oz cornflower and a little milk
600 mls/1 pint water
1 lemon
whipped cream to serve

🍂 Finely grate the rind of one orange and then squeeze the juice from all three oranges.

🍂 Put into a saucepan with the caster and loaf sugar and the half cup of water. Place over a low heat to dissolve the sugar, skim and cook for 10 minutes. Put aside.

🍂 Mix the cornflower to a smooth cream with a little milk and add the 600 mls/ pint of water. Bring to the boil then slowly stir into the saucepan of orange. Add the strained juice of the lemon and allow to simmer for 5 minutes.

🍂 Strain into a wetted mould and leave to set. When cold, turn out onto a dish and serve with whipped cream.

Mary, who really was quite contrary, would have winced at this title. Nevertheless, I can't quite remember which of my guests pronounced this to have a "heavenly taste" but ever since that's what it has been called. Mary would have considered this exaggerated pride. Oh well, so be it!!

Heavenly Pudding

50g/2oz butter
50g/2oz caster sugar
1 egg, size 2
100g/4oz plain flour
5 mls/1 teaspoon baking powder
45 mls/3 tablespoons milk
a little grated lemon rind
30 mls/2 tablespoons of really good jam (I use a cherry and brandy conserve) or honey

🍂 Cream the butter and sugar together until light and fluffy.

🍂 Whisk the egg and slowly add to the butter and sugar.

🍂 Sieve the flour and baking powder and fold into the mixture with the milk and lemon rind.

🍂 Put a layer of jam at the bottom of a 2 pint pudding basin, then pour in the mixture. Cover with greaseproof paper and tinfoil, secure with string and steam for about $^3/_4$ hour until lightly set.

🍂 Leave for 5 minutes at room temperature to firm up then turn out onto a serving dish. Serve with a light white cinnamon sauce.

Only the Reverend "High Church" Collins could have given this very ordinary, stick-to-the-ribs suet pudding such an exalted name.

High Church Pudding

100g/4oz suet
100g/4oz plain flour
breakfast cup of milk
5 mls/1 teaspoon bicarbonate of soda
45 mls/3 tablespoons golden syrup

🍵 Mix all the ingredients together and half fill a 600 ml/1 pint pudding mould.

🍵 Cover with greaseproof paper and tinfoil and secure with string.

🍵 Steam for $2\frac{1}{2}$ hours and serve hot with cream or custard.

Honeycomb Mould

2 eggs, size 2
15g/$\frac{1}{2}$oz gelatine
600 mls/1 pint milk
75g/3oz caster sugar
juice of 2 lemons

Separate the eggs and thoroughly whisk the yolks. Add the sugar and gelatine to the milk, stirring regularly to melt the gelatine.

🍵 Pour the milk over the beaten yolks. Stir well and pour back into the pan. Bring to the boil, stirring constantly. Leave the mixture to cool.

🍵 Whisk the egg whites to a stiff froth and gently fold them into the milk and egg yolk mixture. Add the lemon juice and fold well together. Pour into a $1\frac{1}{2}$ pint mould and leave to cool and set. This is delicious served with tiny shortbread biscuits.

Rice Flummery

600 mls/1 pint milk
strip of lemon peel
1 inch cinnamon stick
50g/2oz caster sugar
75g/3oz ground rice
25g/1oz butter
4 drops almond essence

🍵 Bring the milk, with the lemon peel and cinnamon stick, just to boiling point. Remove the peel and cinnamon and then add the sugar and stir until dissolved.

🍵 Mix the ground rice with a little cold milk and stir into the hot milk. Add the butter and essence. Cook gently, stirring all the time, until the mixture thickens and leaves the sides of the saucepan.

🍵 Pour into a wetted mould and leave until cold. Turn out onto a serving plate and serve with fresh fruit, jam or cream.

This was one of Mrs. Bennet's favourite puddings. Cook would have been hard pressed to get sufficient of these to the side table still piping hot!

Quick Rhubarb Tansy

450g/1lb rhubarb

100g/4oz butter

2 egg yolks

150 mls/$^1/_4$ pint double cream

50g/2oz caster sugar

30 mls/2 tablespoons lemon juice

❦ Prepare and chop the rhubarb into 1 inch pieces. Simmer gently in the butter until cooked.

❦ Whilst this is happening, whisk the egg yolks and lightly whip the cream. Fold both into the rhubarb when it is cooked.

❦ Sweeten to taste and simmer the mixture gently until it is barely firm.

❦ Turn out immediately into a serving dish. Sprinkle with a little caster sugar and the lemon juice and brown under the grill.

Apple Tansy

2 medium sized tart cooking apples

2 dessertspoons unsalted butter

3 egg yolks (size 2)

2 dessertspoons of Rose Water or Rose Hip Syrup

2.5 mls/$^1/_2$ teaspoon grated nutmeg

2 dessertspoons caster sugar

3 egg whites

❦ Peel, core and slice the apples. Heat the butter in a frying pan and fry the apple slices until just soft.

❦ Beat together the egg yolks with 2 dessertspoons of water, the rose water (or Rose Hip Syrup) nutmeg and sugar in a basin.

❦ Whisk the egg whites separately until stiff (but not dry). Fold the whites into the yolk mixture. Tip the whole batter mixture very gently over the apples and fry the underside until set. While it is cooking light the grill and as soon as the underside is set slide the pan under the grill to lightly brown the top.

❦ The difficult part is to fold this light tansy in half with the apples inside when it has cooked, rather like an omelette. The best way is to have a warmed sheet of foil or greased greaseproof paper ready and carefully invert the whole pan onto it. Then lift up one side to fold the tansy. Dredge with caster sugar before serving.

Tea with the Bennets

This lovely country pudding is very unusual and full of goodness. It is a great favourite of my family and friends and was inspired by the lovely English autumn hedgerows, full of colourful fruits simply asking to be used. I'm sure Lizzy would have picked pounds of them during her many long walks.

Hedgerow Pudding

🍂 Simply pick as many blackberries, elderberries, rose-hips, sloes, crab apples and any other edible berries from the hedgerows as you can find to make 900g-1.4 kg/2-3 lbs in weight.

🍂 Simmer together in 600-900mls/1-1¹/₂ pints of water over a gentle heat until the crab apples and sloes are soft. Strain the fruit, add a little rosehip syrup and sweeten to taste.

🍂 Grate about 450g/1lb of bread or cake into crumbs.

🍂 Butter an ovenproof dish and layer it alternately with the fruit mixture and crumbs to make 4-6 layers, finishing with a layer of crumbs.

🍂 Bake in the oven for 1 hour at about 350°F/180°C/Gas Mark 4. Sprinkle with brown sugar and return to the top of the oven or place under the grill to crisp.

🍂 Serve hot or cold, preferably with fresh cream.

This was one of my father's favourite dishes. Mr Bennet would certainly have enjoyed it - sweetness with a hidden spicey twist of humour. Great fun for a dinner party dessert.

Father's Favourite Pudding

3 large cooking apples

25g/1oz caster sugar

2 eggs

300ml/¹/₂ pint milk

5 mls/1 tspn marigold petals

5 mls/1 tspn sweet thyme

5 mls/1 tspn sage

1 green peppercorn, crushed

50g/2oz butter

🍂 Peel and core the apples and cut into rings.

🍂 Whisk the eggs in the milk and sugar and season with the marigold, thyme, sage and peppercorn.

🍂 Put the mixture in a shallow 8in. buttered dish and carefully place the apple rings over the top. Dot with small pieces of butter.

🍂 Bake in a good oven (375°F/ 190°C/Gas Mark 5) for 20-25 minutes.

Dry Measures

1 US cup	= 50g	= 2oz of:	breadcrumbs, cake crumbs	
1 US cup	= 90g	= $3^1/_2$oz of:	ground almonds	
1 US cup	= 100g	= 4oz of:	grated hard cheese, suet icing sugar, flaked almonds	
1 US cup	= 125g	= 5oz of:	white flour, (plain or self-raising)	
1US cup	= 150g	= $5^1/_2$oz of:	wholemeal flour, raisins cornflower	
1 US cup	= 175g	= 6oz of:	mixed peel, sultanas	
1 US cup	= 200g	= 7oz of:	caster sugar, soft brown sugar demerara sugar, long grain rice	
1 US cup	= 300g	= 11oz of:	marmalade	
1 US cup	= 350g	= 12oz of:	jam, syrup, treacle	

Butter, Lard, & Margarine

$^1/_4$ stick		= 25g	= 1oz
1 stick ($^1/_2$ US cup)		= 100g	= 4oz
4 sticks (2 US cups)		= 450g	= 1lb

Liquid Measures

$^2/_3$ US cup	= 150mls	= $^1/_4$ pint
$1^1/_4$ US cups	= 300mls	= $^1/_2$ pint
$2^1/_2$US cups	= 600mls	= 1 pint

Page 6   *On table, back (left to right):* ~
Soda Bread, Everyday Scones, Wednesday Scones, Cheese Muffins
Front (left to right):
Sunday Scones, Crumpets

Page 14   *Clockwise from top right:* ~
Granny's Cheese Pudding, Faggotty Loaf, Cheese Straws, Hedgerow Pudding, Mr. Wickham's 'Indelicate Pudding', Potato Scones

Page 20   *Clockwise from top left:* ~
Cherry Cake, Shearing Cake, Honey Buns, Rich Chocolate Cake, 'Lady Catherine de Bourgh's' Brittle Bites, Meryton Market Squares, Shepherd's Purse, Boiled Fruit Cake

Page 22   *Rich Chocolate Cake*

Page 23   *Shearing Cake*

Page 32   *Clockwise from top left:* ~
Elderflower, Lime or Lemon Posset, Apricot Cream, Green Apple Fool, Baked Figs, Orange Shape

Cook's Notes

Cook's Notes

My sincere thanks to everyone who has contributed in so many ways in helping me to write this book.

To my family and friends for their loving encouragement, my staff at King John's Hunting Lodge Tea Room in Lacock for their support.

To Jill Williams for her endless patience in helping to test many of the recipes (my apologies for her frequently burnt fingers!)

To Tom for his tolerance at my inability to conquer the wordprocessor, so leaving him to take care of all the typing.

To Julie and Stan from Bishopdale Antiques in Leyburn, North Yorkshire for the loan of their beautiful china.

And to Caroline and Duncan for their confidence and encouragement, without which I would never have finished this book.

Margaret Vaughan.

First published 1996.

ISBN 1 86123 065 6.

Printed and bound in England.

Copyright © Margaret Vaughan.

Index